GARTH THE

and other stories

By Brian Ogden

Illustrated by Trudi Webb

By the same author:

The *Maximus Mouse* series
Short Tails and Tall Stories
Angel Alert
Bible Dads and Lads
An Alien for Christmas
Hand in Hand
All published by Scripture Union

The *On the Story Mat* series
Starting Together
News and Tell
Nursery Rhyme Nativities
All published by The Bible Reading Fellowship

Published by
The Leprosy Mission International 2003
© Brian Ogden

All rights and subsidiary rights have been granted to
The Leprosy Mission International
80 Windmill Road, Brentford
Middlesex, TW8 0QH, United Kingdom

Edited and distributed by TLM Trading Limited,
The Leprosy Mission's trading company,
P.O.Box 212
Peterborough PE2 5GD
Phone: 01733 239252   Fax: 01733 239258
Email: enquiries@tlmtrading.com

Editorial and design by Craft Plus Publishing Ltd.
53 Crown Street, Brentwood, Essex, CM14 4BD

Printed and bound in Spain by Bookprint, S.L., Barcelona
A catalogue record for this book is available from the British Library
ISBN 0-902731-50-5

GARTH
THE GIRAFFE

and other stories

To teachers and group leaders –
please feel free to photocopy any of the pictures
in this book for the children to colour.

CONTENTS

GARTH THE GIRAFFE

It was a hot day at Wicken Green School.
The children had finished eating lunch and
some of them were playing football.
David scored a goal.
David waved his arms in the air.
"I am the great-est," chanted David.
"I don't need any of you on my team. I can win
all by myself. Nobody's as good as me."

The other boys and girls looked very fed up.
They saw Mrs Wright, their favourite dinner
lady, and ran over to her.
"Tell us a story, please, Mrs Wright," they said.
"I will if you come and sit under the story tree,"
said Mrs Wright.
The story tree is a nice shady tree on the edge
of the playground, at Wicken Green School.
"I'll tell you a story about Garth the giraffe,"
said Mrs Wright.

"Garth thought he was better than anyone else.
He looked down on everybody. Well, if you are
a giraffe you do look down on everybody.
Garth thought he was so special that he didn't
need any friends.

One day Garth went for a walk by the
acacia trees.
He stopped and took a bite from the branches
at the top.
'We giraffes are truly magnificent animals,' said
Garth to himself.
'There is no animal to touch us.'
And he lifted his head even higher.

Garth was very pleased with himself.
He forgot to look down.
In front of him was a pool of water.
Lots of animals came to the pool for a drink.
The edge of the pool was very muddy.
The mud was very slippery.
In next to no time the pool was full of giraffe.
Garth had slipped into the pool.
His legs stuck out in different directions.
Garth could not move.
Garth badly needed someone to help him.

Rowena the hyena came down to the pool to
drink.
Rowena couldn't believe her eyes.
The pool was full of giraffe.
'I say,' said Garth, 'do you think you could help
me? I'm sort of stuck.'

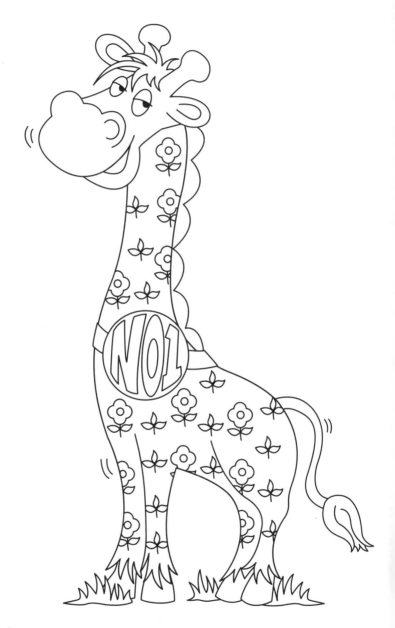

'What sort of stuck?' asked Rowena.
'The sort that means I need help,' said Garth unhappily. 'Please would you get someone to help me?'
'Yes,' said Rowena, 'I'll go and look for somebody at once.'

Rowena ran off quickly.
Soon she found Fino the rhino.
Fino was chewing some grass.
'Excuse me,' said Rowena, 'but I'm looking for a very strong animal to help me.'
'They don't come any stronger than me,' said Fino.

At the pool they found Kate the snake.
She had come for a drink.
'Kate,' said Rowena, 'please help us to rescue Garth, he's stuck.'
Kate carefully crawled out along one of Garth's legs.
She tied the front end of herself around Garth's tummy.
Fino took hold of Kate's tail.
'Heave!' shouted Rowena.
Fino dug his feet into the mud and started to pull.

Slowly, very slowly, Fino
dragged Garth to the edge of
the pond.
At last Garth could stand
up again.
    'Thank you,' said Garth.
        'I was wrong. I really do
need other animals to be my friends.'"

"And Garth," said Mrs Wright, "never thought
he was better than other animals again."
"Thank you for the story, Mrs Wright," said the
children.
"Yes, thank you," said David, as he ran off to
play football again. "Do you want me to go in
goal this time?" asked David.
And Mrs Wright heard him and smiled.

━━━━━━━━━

Heavenly Father,
Sometimes we think we can do things
better than other people. Teach us that
we all need each other.
Amen.

━━━━━━━━━

MACARONI THE PONY

It was dinner time at Wicken Green School.
The Reception and Year One class had just
finished eating lunch.

"Sarah, please take your tray to the trolley,"
said Mrs Wright, the dinner lady.
Sarah looked at the dirty tray.
There was custard and gravy on it.
"Yuck!" thought Sarah and she ran off with the
other children.

Mrs Wright stopped her by the door.
"Sarah, please take your tray to the trolley,"
she said again.
"No!" said Sarah.
"Sarah! Take your tray to the trolley
now, please."

Sarah looked at Mrs Wright. She got her tray
and banged it down on top of the others.
"Oh Sarah, you have made me feel sad," said
Mrs Wright. "As it's wet play today, I'll see you
in your classroom in a minute."

"Tell us a story, please, Mrs Wright," said the children as their favourite dinner lady came into the classroom later.
"I'll tell you a story about Macaroni," said Mrs Wright.

"Macaroni is a pony.
Macaroni is like all ponies.
He likes to have his own way.
He can be very stubborn.
Macaroni's owner is called John.
One day John went into a shop.
Macaroni waited outside.
It was a hot day and John was a long time.
When John came out of the shop he was carrying a big bag.
He tried to lift the bag on to Macaroni's back.
Macaroni jumped to one side.
The bag fell on the floor.

'We need to take this bag home,' said John.
'Please help me to carry it.'
John lifted the bag up again.
Macaroni kicked out with his back legs.
John dropped the bag.

'Macaroni, please help me,'
asked John.
'We need to take this bag home.
I can't do it without you.'
John lifted the bag again.
This time Macaroni let John put it
on his back.
Just as John was tying on the bag
Macaroni ran off down the road.

When Macaroni came to a bridge he stopped.
And, do you know what he did next?
He kicked up his back legs.
The bag went up in the air.
It fell off the bridge.
And it fell into the river with a big splash.
Then, Macaroni ran off home.
John followed him.

Soon Macaroni was feeling hungry.
He went to John for some food.
'I suppose you're hungry,' said John.
'Your food is right where you left it!
It's in the river!
You see I told you that we needed the bag at
home!' said John.
'You really mustn't be so stubborn.'

And Macaroni had to go all the way back to the river to get his food," said Mrs Wright.

"That was a funny story," said Sarah.
"I'm sorry about the tray at dinner time,
Mrs Wright. I didn't mean to be silly."
And Mrs Wright smiled. She knew that Sarah would remember her story about Macaroni.

———

Father God,
Help us not to be stubborn. When we want our own way teach us that you always know what is best for us.
Amen.

BLEAT THE SHEEP

It was a wet and windy day.
A wet play day.
The children were sitting eating their lunch in
the school dining hall.
"I don't like the wind – it nearly blows me
over!" said Emily.
"I don't like the rain – it makes me wet!"
said Edward.
"I don't like fish fingers – they make me choke!"
said Jason.
"I don't like custard – it's all yellow!"
said Anna.
Mrs Wright, the dinner lady, heard what the
children were saying.

After lunch the children went to their classroom
with Mrs Wright.
"Tell us a story, please, Mrs Wright," they said.
"I will when you're sitting down," said
Mrs Wright.
"I'll tell you a story about Bleat the sheep."

"Bleat lived in a large field.
He lived with his mother Eunice.

He lived with his father Rameses.
He lived with his brother Lambo.
And he lived with his sister Lambretta.
The grass was long and green in Bleat's field.
There were no wild animals to chase the sheep.
In fact, there was just about everything a sheep
could want.

But Bleat wasn't happy.
Bleat whinged and moaned about everything.
Bleat whinged if the sun was shining.

'I don't like it when it's hot,' he whinged.
'It makes the grass dry up.'
Bleat whinged if it was raining.
'I don't like getting wet,' whinged Bleat.
'My wool gets soggy.'
Bleat whinged if the wind was blowing.
'I don't like the wind,' he whinged.
'It makes my wool untidy.'
Bleat whinged about the grass.
'This grass isn't very green,' he whinged.
'I shall get tummy ache, I'm sure.'
Bleat whinged when the sheep dog came into
the field.
'The sheep dog's got big teeth,' he whinged.
'He's going to bite me, I'm sure.'
Lambo and Lambretta made up a song about
their brother Bleat.

> 'Bleat, Bleat, white sheep,
> You really make us cringe,
> Yes sir, yes sir,
> All you do is whinge.'

Bleat told his mother and father about the
song. 'They shouldn't sing things like that.
I don't like it.'
'Well stop whinging about things,' said Eunice.

'You should be happy with what you've got,' said Rameses.
Bleat thought about it.
'Perhaps I do whinge too much,' said Bleat."

"And Bleat tried very hard not to whinge anymore," said Mrs Wright.
"Thank you for the story," said the children, "now we'll try not to whinge too!"
And, do you know what?
While the children had been listening to the story it had actually stopped raining!

Loving Father,
You have given us so much – our families and friends, our homes and health.
Help us to remember this when we whinge and moan.
Amen.

TYPHOON THE BABOON

The children were in the playground after lunch.
They were kicking a ball about.
Joshua took a big kick at the ball.
The ball took off like a bird.
It flew straight into the story tree –
and there it stuck.

"I'll get it," said Daniel from Year Three.
"We should tell Mrs Wright," said Joshua.
"I'm best at climbing trees," shouted Daniel.
Daniel ran to the tree.
"See how good I am," shouted Daniel.
He climbed onto the lowest branch.
He climbed onto the next branch and then
the next…
But the ball was higher still.
Daniel started to feel a bit nervous.

Mrs Wright, the dinner lady, could see what
was happening.
Climbing trees in the playground was against
school rules.
"Stay where you are Daniel," said Mrs Wright,
"and don't move!"

"Mr Jiggins is coming with his ladder to get you down," she called.
Mr Jiggins is the caretaker at Wicken Green School.
Soon Daniel was on the ground again.

Mrs Wright told all the children to sit under the story tree.
"What Daniel did was very wrong," said Mrs Wright.
"Now I want you to listen to a story.
It's a story about Typhoon the baboon."

"Typhoon the baboon was always boasting about what he could do.
'I can climb higher than you can,' he told Priscilla the gorilla.
'I can climb to the moon!'
'I can run faster than you,' he told Garth the giraffe.
'I can run faster than a train.'
'I can carry more than you,' he told Banjul the mule.
'I can carry you and all your bags!'

The other animals got tired of Typhoon boasting all the time.

'I'll tell you what,' said Priscilla the gorilla.
'Can you see that tall tree over there?'
'Yes,' said Typhoon.
'Do you see the branch at the top?'
asked Priscilla.
'Yes,' said Typhoon.
'I don't think you can climb up and sit on that branch,' said Priscilla.
'Oh yes I can,' said Typhoon.
'I can climb anything.'

Typhoon ran over to the tree.
The first few metres were easy.
There were lots of big branches.
'This is simple,' said Typhoon.
'I could do this with my eyes shut.'
'I think I should keep them open,' said Priscilla.

Typhoon climbed higher and higher.
'Can you still see me?' asked Typhoon.
'Yes,' said Priscilla, 'we can still see you.'
'I'm nearly there,' said Typhoon.
'Keep going,' said Priscilla.
Typhoon stopped climbing and looked down.
'A little further,' said Priscilla.
Typhoon didn't move.
'I don't like it,' he said.

'I can't go any higher.
HELP!' shouted Typhoon.
'I'm stuck.'

"It took Priscilla and her friends a long time to
get Typhoon down," said Mrs Wright.
'Oh dear,' said Typhoon when he came back
to earth.
'Perhaps baboons should keep their paws on the
ground where they belong.'"

"Sometimes we boast about things that we
think we can do," said Mrs Wright.
"It often gets us into trouble, doesn't it Daniel?"

Dear God,
When I feel like boasting about how good
I am, help me to remember that every
thing I have, and everything I can do,
comes from you.
Amen.

SQUIRM THE WORM

Mrs Wright, the dinner lady, lives a long way
from Wicken Green School.
It takes her a long time to walk to school
every morning – and then back home again
every afternoon.
"I know," said Mrs Wright, "I'll buy a bicycle.
All the children ride bicycles.
I'm sure I can ride one if I do my best."

Soon her bicycle came.
It was bright red.
It had a big basket on the front for shopping.
"What a lovely bicycle," said Mrs Wright.
"I shall soon be riding it to school."

Mrs Wright put on her new red cycle helmet.
Then she climbed on to her new red bicycle.
She sat down on the saddle.
Mrs Wright put one foot on the pedal.
She pushed her foot down.
The bicycle wobbled.
Mrs Wright wobbled.
The red bicycle stopped.
"It isn't as easy as I thought," said Mrs Wright.

"Perhaps it will be easier after a cup of tea."
She lent the bicycle against the fence.
She made a cup of tea.

"Now, I must try again,"
said Mrs Wright a little
later. Once more she sat on
the saddle.
Once more she put her foot on the pedal.
Once more the bicycle wobbled.
And once more Mrs Wright wobbled.
"Oh dear," she said, "the children make it look
so easy when they ride to school."
That morning Mrs Wright pushed her bike all
the way to school.
The children saw her pushing her bicycle.
After dinner the children sat under the story
tree. They were waiting for Mrs Wright.
"Tell us a story, please, Mrs Wright," they said.
"I'll tell you a story about a worm," said
Mrs Wright.

"The worm's name is Squirm.
Squirm the worm lives in my garden.
He lives under the earth.
It isn't easy being a worm.
Sometimes you bump into things underground.

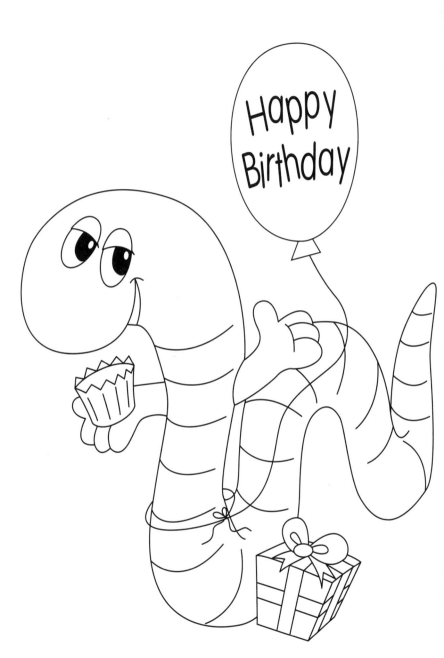

One day Squirm thought he would like to see his friend called Arthur Worm.
Arthur was a rather short worm.
On this day it was Arthur's birthday and he was having a party.
Arthur lives on the other side of the garden.

Squirm started his journey.
Soon he bumped into the roots of a tall tree.
Tall trees have big roots.
Squirm wriggled round one root.
He wriggled under the next one.
But there was still another one.
'Oh dear,' said Squirm, 'I shall never get to Arthur's house.
I must try harder.'

After a struggle he left the tree roots behind.
He wriggled on another few metres.
'OUCH!' said Squirm.
Poor Squirm had hit his head on a big rock.
'Oh dear,' said Squirm, 'I shall never get to Arthur's house.
I must try harder.'
He tried wriggling under the rock – but it was too deep.
He tried wriggling over it – but it was too high.

He tried going round the left side of the rock – but it was too wide.
'Oh dear,' said Squirm, 'I shall never get to Arthur's house.
I think I shall give up and go home.'
Then he thought about the acorn cup cakes.
And he thought about the birthday mud pie.
'I want to go to Arthur's party,' said Squirm.
'I'll try again. I'll really do my best this time.'
This time he tried the right side of the rock.
This time nothing stopped him.

"Arthur and Squirm had a lovely party," said Mrs Wright. "And all because Squirm didn't give up. Because he did his best."
"Don't give up trying to ride your bicycle," said the children.
"Just do your best and you'll manage it."
And soon Mrs Wright was able to cycle safely to school on her red bicycle.

Dear Jesus,
Sometimes it's very hard to keep on trying. When I feel like giving up help me to remember that you never gave up.
Amen.

TWEEDLEDEE THE CHIMPANZEE

It was Mrs Wright's birthday.
The children came to see her in the playground.
They gave Mrs Wright a parcel.
"Thank you," they said, "for all the lovely
stories that you tell us."

The parcel was wrapped in pretty paper.
Mrs Wright took off the paper.
Inside was a great big box of chocolates.
There were strawberry chocolates.
There were toffee chocolates.
There were chocolates with nuts.
There were lots of chocolates.
"Thank you," said Mrs Wright.
"I love chocolates. Thank you very much, that
was a lovely surprise."

The children ran off to play.
Mrs Wright stood by the story tree.
"I think I might have one chocolate now,"
she said.
Mrs Wright chose a toffee chocolate.
It was sweet and chewy and...

"Perhaps I'll try one more," said Mrs Wright.
This time she chose a strawberry chocolate.
It was soft and gooey and …
"I think I've got room for another one," said
Mrs Wright.
This time she chose a nutty chocolate.
Before long Mrs Wright had eaten half the
chocolates in the box.
She shut the lid.
"Oh dear," she said, "I have been rather greedy."

The children ran over to her.
"Did you like your present?" they asked.
"Yes, thank you," said Mrs Wright.
"I think I liked it too much."

"Tell us a story, please, Mrs Wright," said the
children.
The children sat down under the story tree.
"I'll tell you a story about Tweedledee," said
Mrs Wright.

"Tweedledee was a chimpanzee.
Tweedledee was a rather greedy chimpanzee.
'Tweedledee,' said his mother, 'you really
mustn't eat so much.
It's not good for you.'

33

But Tweedledee took no notice of his mother.
He ate all the food he could find.
He swallowed bananas.
He chewed leaves.
He nibbled termites, which are a bit like ants.
He munched eggs.
And Tweedledee got larger and larger.

One day he saw some mangoes.
Mangoes are a lovely fruit.
The mangoes were growing in a garden.
Round the garden was a fence.
In the fence was a hole.
Tweedledee squeezed through the hole.
He ate lots of mangoes.

A man came into the garden.
He shouted at Tweedledee.
Tweedledee ran to the fence.
But he couldn't get through the hole.
He couldn't go forwards.
He couldn't go backwards.
He was really stuck.
The man had to help him.
'Don't take my mangoes again,' said the man.
'Don't be so greedy and then you won't
get stuck.'"

"Being greedy can get you into trouble," said Mrs Wright.
"Please help me eat my chocolates," she said to the children.
"You see, I don't want to get stuck either!"

———

Father God,
You made us and you know what's best
for us. Help us not to be greedy but to
look after our bodies. Most of all, help us
to remember those who have much
less than us.
Amen.

DOMINGO THE FLAMINGO

Mrs Wright saw Aaron standing by himself in
the playground.
Aaron isn't very tall.
In fact Aaron is very short.
Aaron looked very unhappy.

"Hello, Aaron," said Mrs Wright.
"Haven't you got anyone to play with?"
"No!" said Aaron sadly.
"Why's that?" asked Mrs Wright.
"They all laugh at me," said Aaron.
"Why do they laugh at you?"
"They laugh at me because I'm not very tall.
They call me names like Titch and Shorty,"
said Aaron.
"That's not very kind," said Mrs Wright.

Just then the other children came up to
Mrs Wright.
"We're hot and tired. Will you tell us a story,
please, Mrs Wright?" they said.
"I will if you sit down under the shady story
tree," said Mrs Wright.
The children all sat down.

"I'll tell you a story about a flamingo.
The flamingo's name was Domingo," said
Mrs Wright.

"Flamingos live in very large flocks.
Flamingos, as you know, have long legs.
But Domingo didn't have long legs.
Domingo's legs were rather short.
The other flamingos used to tease Domingo.
'Don't stand in deep water,' they said.
'You might drown.'

Domingo was a very unhappy flamingo.
He didn't want to be different from the other
flamingos – but it was how he had been born.
From the moment he had crawled out of his
egg his legs had been shorter than all the
other flamingos.
There was nothing he could do about it.

The other flamingos kept on teasing him.
'Why don't you wear high heeled shoes?'
they said.
Domingo the flamingo became very unhappy.
The other flamingos even made up a poem
about him.

'Flamingos are tall
Domingo is small,
If his legs were shorter –
He'd be under water!'

The other flamingos thought the poem was
very funny.

'I'm just the same as everyone else,'
said Domingo.
'It's just that I'm not quite as tall.'"

Mrs Wright looked at the children.
"Now, what do think about that story?" asked
Mrs Wright.
"I think the other flamingos were really mean to
Domingo," said David.
"They shouldn't have teased him," said Joshua,
"just because he was a bit shorter."
"I think he needs some friends," said Esther.
"And I think you're right," said Mrs Wright.
"It is always unfair to tease someone because
they are different."
"That was a good story," said the children.
"Come on Aaron, let's play another game."
And this time Aaron went off happily to play
with the others.

Heavenly Father,
Thank you for making us. Help us to
understand that some people are different
from us. And help us to remember
that you made us all and we are all
equally special.
Amen.

BOISTEROUS THE RHINOCEROS

It was a very hot day.
Most of the children had finished lunch.
They were sitting in the shade under the
story tree.

Suddenly a quiet afternoon turned into a very
noisy one.
The noise came from Nathan.
Nathan was jumping about.
Nathan was kicking an empty drink can.
Nathan was shouting at the other children.
Nathan was always excited about something.
Sometimes he was called Noisy Nathan.

Mrs Wright walked over towards the story tree.
"Hello, Mrs Wright!" shouted Nathan, in a very
loud voice.
"Nathan," said Mrs Wright, "please come and
sit down with the others."
"Tell us a story, please, Mrs Wright," said
the children.
"I will when you're all sitting down – quietly!"
said Mrs Wright.

"I will tell you a story about a rhinoceros.
The name of the rhinoceros was Boisterous."

"Boisterous was a very noisy rhinoceros.
Boisterous liked to shout at other animals.
Boisterous liked to play tricks on other animals.
Boisterous often got very excited.
It was then that Boisterous did silly things.

One day, Boisterous thought he would play a
trick on James.
James is an elephant.
Only silly animals play tricks on elephants.
Boisterous hid behind some bushes by the side
of the path.
On the other side of the path there is a muddy
pond.
James walked down the path every day.
Boisterous thought it would be funny if James
fell in the pond.

Boisterous saw James coming.
As James went past, the rhinoceros bounced out
from the bushes.
Boisterous shouted at the top of his big
rhinoceros voice.
James jumped with surprise.

But James didn't fall in the pond.
James fell on top of Boisterous!
Boisterous tried to get out of the way.
Not even a rhinoceros wants an elephant falling
on him.
As he moved out of the way, he slipped into
the pond.
There was another loud shout.
It came from a very wet and muddy Boisterous.

Later that day the other animals came to
see Boisterous.
He was still covered in thick brown mud.
Garth the giraffe was the first to speak.
'Boisterous, we like you, but we wish you would
calm down.'
'Please try to be a little quieter,' said
Tweedledee the chimpanzee.
'Just stay cool,' said Typhoon the baboon.

Boisterous looked at all his friends.
'Sorry,' he said.
'I really will try not to get so over-excited.'"

"It wasn't easy for Boisterous," said Mrs Wright.
"But he tried hard to change and soon he took
everything more calmly."

"That was a good story," said Nathan.
"Perhaps I could be like Boisterous.
Like he was at the end of the story – that is!"
The other children laughed and they all ran off
to play together quietly. Well, fairly quietly!

———

Father God,
Sometimes we get too excited and noisy.
It's then that we do silly things that can
hurt others. Help us to live our lives in a
way that pleases you so that we don't
hurt other people.
Amen.

CACKLE THE JACKAL

It was playtime and the children were in the playground.
Mrs Wright, the dinner lady, was in the playground with them.
Some of the children were playing football.
Others were playing with a skipping rope.
Most of the children were playing nicely.

But Abigail wasn't playing very nicely at all.
Abigail took the skipping rope from Molly and ran off with it.
Abigail caught the football and kicked it out of the playground.
She ran into Ethan and knocked him over.
Ethan started to cry.
"You're just a big baby," shouted Abigail.
"Abigail," said Mrs Wright, "come and stand by me, please."
Abigail stood next to Mrs Wright.

"Abigail, I want you to listen to a story," said Mrs Wright.
"The story is about a jackal.
The jackal's name is Cackle.

Cackle isn't a very good jackal.
Every day Cackle goes to jackal school.
Cackle is the biggest jackal in her class.
She is stronger than the other jackals.
She is taller than the other jackals.
Everyday, at playtime, Cackle does very
naughty things.

One day she went over to Raquel.
Raquel was eating a bar of chocolate.
Cackle snatched the chocolate away from her.
Cackle ate some of the chocolate.
Raquel said, 'That's my chocolate.
Please give it back to me.'
Cackle just laughed.
'It's my chocolate now,' she said.
'Try and get it back.'
Raquel held out her paw.
Cackle just grabbed her paw and pushed
Raquel over.

Raquel started to cry.
'You're just a baby, Raquel,' said Cackle.
Raquel looked very unhappy.
'You're just a bully,' said Raquel.
'It's easy fighting jackals smaller than you.
That's what bullies do.'"

"But Cackle just ran off eating the rest of Raquel's chocolate," said Mrs Wright.

Mrs Wright looked at Abigail.
Abigail was looking at the floor.
"What do you think about that story, Abigail?" asked Mrs Wright.
It seemed a long time before Abigail answered.
"Cackle was really horrid to Raquel," whispered Abigail.
"She was a bully and she stole her chocolate."

"It's easy to be a bully but much harder to be kind," said Mrs Wright.
The whistle blew. Abigail was very thoughtful as she went to line up.
The next time Mrs Wright saw the children she was very pleased to see that Abigail was playing nicely with the others.

———

Father God,
Thank you for all our playtimes. Thank you for friends. Help us always to be kind to other people and never to bully them.
Amen.

———

PARDON THE PYTHON

There was a very loud crash.
The crash came from the other side of the
school dining hall.
Mrs Wright went to look.
On the floor was a pile of broken plates.
It was a dreadful mess.
There were pieces of potato lying in a puddle
of gravy.
There were carrots in a puddle of custard.
There were peas and chips.

Mrs Wright was not very happy.
Nobody came to tell her that they
were sorry for knocking over the plates.
Mrs Wright cleared up the broken plates.
She washed the floor.
She looked out of the window
– it was wet play.

When she went into the classroom the children
were sitting on the carpet looking at books.
"Tell us a story, please, Mrs Wright," they said.
Mrs Wright thought about the mess she had just
cleared up...

"I'll tell you a story about a python," she said.
"A python is a snake that can grow to be
several metres long. My story is about a python
called Pardon."

"Pardon the python was a rather careless and
clumsy python. She never seemed to know what
her tail was doing.
Sometimes her head would be on dry ground
whilst her tail was in a muddy pond.
When she went home she left muddy marks all
over the carpet.

Pardon's parents used to get quite cross.
'Pardon,' they said, 'please take care.
Try to remember that your tail is always
behind you.'
'I'm sure it wasn't my fault,' said Pardon, 'it
was an accident.'

The next day Pardon went to the supermarket
to do some shopping.
Pardon liked shopping.
Pardon put the shopping in the trolley.
There were bags of buns, packets of powder,
boxes of biscuits, cartons of cream and cans
of custard.

Soon the trolley was quite full.
Pardon liked to ride on the trolley.
She liked to hang on the handle and push the
trolley with her tail.
Soon she was going quite fast.
She pushed past the pets' food.
She whizzed past the washing powder
She raced round the ready-meals.
She flew past the freezers.
She dashed past the delicatessen.
She sprinted past the soups –
And CRASHED into a pyramid of cans.
The cans went everywhere.

The Manager came to see Pardon.
'Have you anything to say for yourself?' asked
the Manager.
'I'm really very sorry,' said Pardon.
'It was all my fault. I was being a bit careless.
Can I help you to clear up?'
The Manager looked at Pardon.
'As you are sorry,' said the Manager, 'I won't do
anything else about it.
But please take more care next time.'"

The children were very quiet when Mrs Wright finished her story.

Then Joseph stood up.

"I'm really sorry, Mrs Wright," he said, "but I knocked all the plates on the floor. I should have come and told you."

Mrs Wright smiled at Joseph.

"Thank you for telling me, Joseph," said Mrs Wright.

"As you are sorry I won't do anything else about it. But if it ever happens again, please come and tell me right away, then we can clear up the mess together."

Father God,
It is hard to say sorry and we aren't very good at it. Please help us to say sorry when we have done wrong things. Thank you that you forgive us when we really are sorry.
Amen.

PENN THE HEN

The children were playing in the playground.
Mrs Wright was watching them.
Sanjeev and Harry were playing football in
one corner.
Jade and Luke were playing animal hospital.
Amber was skipping all around the playground
very fast.

"Amber, please don't skip in and out of the
other children," said Mrs Wright. "It spoils their
games and someone might get hurt."
Amber didn't listen.
"Amber, please go and skip somewhere else,"
said Mrs Wright.
Amber still didn't listen.
She skipped right into the middle of Jade and
Luke's game.
"Ouch!" said Luke, holding his ear. "You hit me
with your skipping rope and it really hurts."

Mrs Wright told all the children to come and
join her under the story tree.
"I think that it's time for a story," said
Mrs Wright.

"I'll tell you a story about a hen.
The hen's name was Penn.
It was short for Penelope."

"Penn the hen lived on a farm.
She lived with a lot of other hens.
Penn the hen wasn't always a very sensible hen.
You see, Penn always thought that she
knew best.

'Hens, please help me by laying your eggs in
the hen house,' said the farmer.
'It is safe here and the wild animals won't be
able to catch you.'
Penn didn't want to listen to the farmer's
good advice.
'I'm not going to sit in that horrid, smelly, old
hut,' clucked Penn.
'I don't want to lay my eggs in the same place
as everyone else.
I'm going to make my nest under this bush.'

Penn collected pieces of straw and some
old feathers.
She built her nest under the bush.
'Penn,' said the farmer, 'please lay your eggs in
the hen house.

Then I shall know that you are safe.
And I shall know where to find your eggs.'
'No,' clucked Penn, refusing to listen to the
farmer. 'I'm staying here.
I'm sure that I know best.'

As the sun went to bed Penn sat on her nest.
The moon tried hard to shine but clouds got in
the way.
Soon it was quite dark.
Penn wasn't sure that she liked the dark all
by herself.
Then she heard a noise.
The noise came from across the farmyard.
It was the sort of noise that only a large
animal makes.
Penn was now quite sure she didn't like the
dark all by herself.

The noise came nearer.
'Oh dear,' clucked Penn, 'I think the farmer was
right.
I should be in the hen house.'
Penn picked up her wings and ran to the
hen house.
'Let me in!' she clucked outside the door.
The other hens were very kind.

They opened the door and let Penn in."

"Penn the hen listened very hard to the farmer's good advice from that day on," said Mrs Wright.

"Thank you, Mrs Wright," said the children.
"That was a good story."
"Amber, would you like to come and play animal hospital with us now?" asked Jade.
"Yes," said Amber. "I'd like that."
And the children ran off.

_____

Father God,
Sometimes we are silly and we don't listen to good advice. Please help us to realise that we don't always know best. Help us to listen to others.
Amen.

SHARE THE HARE

It was a wet playtime.
Mrs Wright went into the classroom.
The children were playing with the toys.
Some of them were in the play house.
Some of them were looking at books.

David was playing with Gizzmo.
Gizzmo is an electronic toy that talks.
Nobody else had a Gizzmo.
David had brought Gizzmo into school for
'Show and Tell' time that afternoon.
"Let's have a go!" begged Patrick.
"No," said David. "Gizzmo is mine."
"Go on," said Anna. "Let me have a go."
"No," said David. "Gizzmo is mine."
"Please," said Rajinder. "Please let me try it."
"No," said David. "He's my Gizzmo – none of
you can have a turn."

The others got tired of watching David.
They saw Mrs Wright and ran over to her.
"Tell us a story, please, Mrs Wright," they said.
"I will when you're sitting down," said
Mrs Wright.

HAIRFIELD UNITED

Mrs Wright saw that David came to sit down
with the other children.

"I'll tell you a story about a hare," she said.
"The hare's name was Share.
His real name was Harold but everyone called
him Share.
This is the story of how Harold got his
new name."

"One morning it started to rain.
By lunchtime it was raining harder.
By teatime it was raining harder still.
By bedtime some of the burrows that the hares
lived in were flooded.

'I don't know what I'm going to do,' said
Hare Twoday.
'My burrow is full of water.'
'You can share my burrow,' said Harold.
Hare Twoday and his family snuggled down in
Harold's burrow for the night.
'I don't know what we're going to do about
breakfast,' said Hare Twoday the next morning.
'Our breakfast is floating around in our
old burrow.'
'You can share my breakfast,' said Harold.

Hare Twoday and his family had a good
breakfast after all.

Later that morning the sun started to shine.
Soon the flooded burrows dried out and Hare
Twoday and his family went home.
'Thank you, Harold, for sharing your home and
your breakfast with us,' said Hare Twoday.

A few days later Harold was playing pawball
with his family.
They were having a great game.
Soon other hares came to watch.
There was Hare Cut, Hare Band, and Hare Slide.
'I wish we could join in the game,' said
Hare Cut.
'Come on then,' said Harold.
'You're very welcome to share our game.'
The others joined in and had a great time.

'Harold,' said Hare Band, 'you're such a good
friend to everyone.
You never mind sharing your
things.'
'I think we should call you Share
the Hare,' said Hare Slide."

"And from that time on he was always called Share," said Mrs Wright.

"Thank you Mrs Wright," said the children, as they ran off to play again.

"Would anyone like to play with Gizzmo?" asked David. "You can have a turn, if you're very careful."

And Patrick was the first.

Loving Father,
You have given us so much – our homes,
our families and our friends. Help us to
share what we have with others.
Amen.